Made Beautiful by Use

To the fantastic Laurie Dawson:

You are an assolutely
unbelievable joy to be around
Hope you find something in these poims
xx
Sean.

Made
Beautiful
by Use

Sean Horlor

[signature]

John Barton, Editor

Signature
EDITIONS

Cover design by Terry Gallagher/Doowah Design.
Cover photo by Anthony Horlor.
Photo of Sean Horlor by Darren St. Laurent.

This book was printed on Ancient Forest Friendly paper.
Printed and bound in Canada by Marquis Book Printing Inc.

We acknowledge the support of The Canada Council for the Arts and the Manitoba Arts Council for our publishing program.

Library and Archives Canada Cataloguing in Publication

Horlor, Sean, 1981–
    Made beautiful by use / Sean Horlor.

Poems.
ISBN 978-1-897109-13-7

    I. Title.

PS8615.O75M33 2007   C811'.6   C2007-901903-X

Signature Editions
P.O. Box 206, RPO Corydon, Winnipeg, Manitoba, R3M 3S7
www.signature-editions.com

For my father Anthony
and in memory of my mother Louise

Table of Contents

Empty Container

St. Brendan the Navigator

The Seven Heavenly Virtues

St. George the Dragon Slayer

Hagiographies

Saints & Patronages

Acknowledgements

Empty Container

"Here is the world, that should be
enough to make you happy."

—Louise Glück, *Meadowlands*

In Praise of Beauty
— after Karen Solie

What we see shapes our imagining.

Poetry, clothes, a pop star's swagger.
    Cologne in glass bottles.

A man with eyes the colour
    Of a eucalyptus leaf turned over.

A spotlight's preference
    For shimmer over shine.

For every act of daring
    The astonished eye chooses to praise.

And for all that drifts: shipwrecks,
    Lightning, a stranger's hello—

Beauty with edge.
    Beauty with consequence.

A kind of grief that separates our lives
    Into all that matters, then all that does not

And all it asks of you
    Is to look, to look twice, to keep looking.

Desire is lonely work.

In Praise of Solitude

Too many people keep telling me
they'd rather do nothing with someone else
than do nothing alone. I'm sure
the stiff-kneed woman
sheered by dumpster shadow
resting against the cardboard bin this afternoon
would also disagree with them—
as she was by herself, seemingly
by choice and comfortable enough to doze
while shaded from what little sun
June had to offer. She looked up
from the pavement after the back door slammed,
her mouth opening. I said no and kept
walking. Though she stared
straight into my eyes, I cut
through the overgrown lot
behind the building and left her watching
the space my body made
after it passed through that field alone.

In Praise of What is Found Again

The sea obeys and fetters break
And lifeless limbs thou dost restore
While treasures lost are found again
When young or old thine aid implore
— *Responsory of St. Anthony*

The newspapers herald
this is the age of the individual.

Weeks pass and disgorge
the lost marginalia of my existence:

keys, that ever-elusive sock's return from AWOL,
a promise ring from years ago

when such symbols could steady the earth
with the pause and lustre of a loose, earthquaked clear.

The present is a contemplation of what is:
bearded men hawking once-upon-a-times,

mis-strung guitars and braided everythings—
the sidewalks studded with beggars,

their empty hats like hearts.
To romantics, Main St. is made beautiful by use:

the dark-carved street during
midsummer brownouts; suspended,

the smog's particulate trumpets
through our lungs. Like fingerprints,

every tongue-print is different.
This is for what comes to us

through language: sunstruck, modern—
a demonstration of gunmetal, of words that gleam.

In Praise of Verse

Too often, you don't feel anything,
come home after a hard day
and walk into the river, hands parting
the heavy water. The rushing
takes what it wants, will even loosen
rock from the wildness on the far shore
as the pines scrape the daylight into dusk.
Once there was a time when you knew
what it meant to be true to an idea.
Swim or don't swim, what you hear
in this river is a question you won't remember
and what you taste in its waters
is another man's mouth
telling you about the night his brother
swallowed four eight-balls of coke
at a roadblock and made it home in time
for his heart to explode on the bathroom floor.

In Praise of Listening

*Behold, I stand at the door, and knock: if any man hear my
voice, and open the door, I will come in to him…*
                                          — *Revelations 3:20*

Sleeping, we let our shadows move like open mouths.
Who's listening?

These hands speak of holding,
of days clapped into being.

Trampling, plush with intent,
it's my voice pounding at the door.

There's naming to do.

Pitch. Timbre. Tone.
The intonation of the word, *Good-bye.*

What did you just hear
unfurling in your ear's delicate rosette?

At first, I believed the man who taught me
sound is vibration.

Our bodies tell us otherwise.

A whistle. A knock.
The unanswered door.

What is possible in this world?

There are moments the human body
amplifies absolutely.

In Praise of Letting Go

An empty container
Can be filled
Let us choose carefully
With what
          "Circle" — Louise Horlor

An empty container, Tupperware, anything
that can be sealed and stay airlocked.
Closed. Clear as driftglass though
with a lid that can be opened
without effort as if to say: what is this?
Something like a day—that

can be filled—on an angle of volcanic rock
where decades of tree growth wash up as they are:
roots intact, seaweed stiff in the breeze.
The marginal tide rubbing smiles into sand.
The algae a different kind of mould, healthy and green
and ready for the ocean's eventual return.

Let us choose carefully then, the general view
and what it means to us, our own
collusive scenery: a homestead,
the measured hush of waves on that beach
farthest from everywhere else, where the dead
are dead, and living this day, let us fill it

with what we choose, carefully, and when at last full
in the way of trees grow around and over
until night leafs into place above
a field with two floodlights and farther
along the horizon, the red feather
of a radio antenna flashing against grey cloud.

St. Brendan the Navigator

"He who seeks, finds."

—Luke 11:10

St. Brendan Sets Sail

There! Their first rigged sail
jigged. The Celtic cross's
first tilt to the sun. The first time the first
son of Finlug bent the wind to his will and believed
it into being. Behind him: his first departure
point, the Ardfert coastline waving
its whitecapped farewell. First missionary
or first marauder? That night,
the fourteen monks manning his crew
ordered their thirsts for Brendan: *first women, then God—*
then every thirst thereafter! Ten days later:
April 1st. No food. No water. Six yards of swell
since the first day of spring, but he hadn't given up
on the rest of the year, so why give up now?
Hours after, the first white rain beyond Ardfert
stilled the wind and green-backed waves.
Then, all at once, herring leapt from the water
to the curragh's slick deck. With every fish
firsthand proof that purpose ordains saintliness.
Firstly. Firstness. First—the absurdity
of that word in all its forms. Everything
always beginning and how
tiring that beginning was: no oars, no wind,
their sails collapsed. The sky stretched overhead
like the palm of an open hand. Every morning
the sun drifted across a sea of their own imagining
into the great unknown that beckoned.

St. Brendan and the Isle of Sheep

Not their first landing here, but the one
after their return, after its hermit
sailed them west where Jasconious,
spawn of Leviathan, relinquished
his great back for Easter Mass.
After they whitened the lamb's fleece
in a caldron of boiling salt water;
after the lesser whales ringed
that floating monster to sing
psalmodies in Brendan's honour.
After the fish congregated alongside
to offer their tithe in a tray of kelp:
two black pearls the size of sheep
eyes. The morning after all that
hallelujah, they returned to the Isle
of Sheep. What first appeared
to be low-moving fog was truly
the flock grazing towards
the harbour shore. In their absence,
one lamb's coat had burled overnight
to the girth of two grown men.
Every good work required sacrifice;
to kill one more lamb would not
diminish that island's plenty.
Yet the hermit said, Its wool is now
a knot of great intricacy, which
cannot be undone by the hands of men.
As proof, the hermit called
the beast and pressed Brendan's hand
against it, saying, The lamb is in the herd.
The lamb is part of its herd.
Yet this lamb is not the herd it belongs to.
So it is with this lamb and its flock,
and so it is with God.

St. Brendan and the Isle of Weeping

The first fountain was still, silty
with the red dust of this place, it incandesced
under the last of the autumn sky like a rusted shield.

Soundless, the next seeped from rock
in a braid of many blues to a pool darker
than the ring around the brown of Brendan's eye.

All around him: wind counting palm fronds,
the tide slipping from the shore.
Forty days sailing without rain—

yet he could not drink from either water.
At dusk, the crickets filled his head with sorrow.
It was then he heard the silence of the two fountains

for what it was: to know the sound of the cricket
in autumn is to know that suffering
in its human form should remain unheard.

St. Brendan and the Isle of Birds

Its rock shore windy and full of wood,
full of rot, full of wanting. Its beach grass in tufts.
Its river narrow and without sand,
without sound—motionless. Its stone salted, and pooled
with water, sunlit, and steaming in the midday.
Downriver and inland, reflected in a spring—
whose water nourished in one swallow—
a white-branched tree grew birds instead of leaves.
Birds: without limit and without end.
Cormorants, blue-eyed and hook-billed; puffins, blood-beaked and
clowning; peregrines keening; hawks rending; gulls scavenging;
osprey diving; storm petrels purring; sparrows surging; peacocks
lifting their feathered skirts; razorbills; vultures; eiders; parrots;
pheasants; gannets; loons; quail—
    To Brendan's bell calling from the ship's foredeck
flew a single dove to rest on the mast: near the bell but not directly to
it. An omen or a warning, the dove returned to flight and the
mechanics of flying, taking wing,
lifting off—

St. Brendan and the Devil

It sat atop the mainsail, growling Brendan knew not what,
until a thistle uncurled from its mouth to speak in tongues
to the monks below. It said, Here is the killick
weighed, your halyards and rigging
stanchioned by spars and the tautest of block and tackle—
By great, grand fathoms, league by uncharted league,
these waters will ebb never-ending to your every heave
to. With a cross for an ensign, by heaven's marque,
what carries you forth, isle by unknown isle,
shall leave you ragged, plundered, pillaged—quartered
by an insatiable thirst for souls, driven to the rope's
end—hull wormed, your hope
hornswoggled, scuppered and scuttled, floundering
through the southernmost doldrums, sails furled,
marooned and forever adrift at sea.

St. Brendan and the Abbot of Clonmacnoise

There were shipes seen in the skyes with their men this yeare.
— Annals of Clonmacnoise (AD 744)

Thirty days into the blackness Brendan
warned them against and tired of the unknown
they dropped the anchor to stop the tether

that drew them westward into paradise.
There was no splash. The ship listed, then jerked
to a halt. Finally in the distance

a beacon lit up, yet Brendan could not
draw the anchor back aboard. So with one
great breath, he slid down the rope to find

the fluke lodged in the altar at Clonmacnoise.
Casting a shadow, the ship drifted above
the monastery like a wooden kite.

The abbot helped sever the anchor
from the line, warning, Stay here and you won't
live long in this land you are crossing.

Breathless in this place astonished sailors
fall to when lost at sea, Brendan climbed skyward
knowing why so many choose to drown.

St. Brendan and the Land of the Blessed

He said, Vine, and ate melons.
He said, Cross, and a white cockatoo passed overhead.
He said, Lake, and his soul's smooth stone skipped across it.

For seven years, indulged by the marvelous,
all that water in water above water,
every island, hermit, bird, fish, whale, devil, cricket
had become something other than what they were,
spoke to him in visions
that demanded interpretation.

He said,

Valley.

Field.

Grape.

How strange that paradise
turned out to be meaningless.

The Seven Heavenly Virtues

"What noun
would you want

spoken on your skin
your whole life through?"

—Mark Doty, *Sweet Machine*

Faith

Watching the rain age this world,
under these words, what do you hear?

All day long, the claxon from a car alarm
keeps wailing and wailing.

As for the fog pooling outside my patio door:
I know it's not what I think

it is because I don't know what to think.
Perhaps Baudrillard was on the right track.

Can what we believe in be
reduced to signs that prove existence?

This morning, the sky
came down to lie against the earth.

Yesterday, a small bird flew in
to the window and broke its neck.

Fortitude

The staircase to the third floor
    is moulding over again, the flowering black
        bloom of a wet summer.

Here is the carpet I always ignore: taupe,
    not red. The only sound this hallway holds
        is my arrival: footfall, uneven with last night's rain.

So the neighbour's son carves
    guns on the wooden railing separating
        our deck. So what.

This morning a grocery bag
    plunged out the window
        chasing after someone's soul.

Life being what it is, sneakers
    dangle from courtyard power cables.
        The hypothetical can be very time-consuming.

Months ago I was cornered by a man
    at the 24-hour Shell station. His bloody knuckles
        marked my shirt with a red wing.

Love, or What should you believe in?

This word would be easier if
I could just say heart
before moving on to the short journey fingers make
between the buttons of a clean shirt—
then fold the heart over until all
that remains is its semblance across this page.
A blueprint. An ink blot. Something
to interpret under another's care:
There is no wrong answer.
Rorschach-inspired, I saw
what I wanted to see:
the shadow of my hand
touching your chest, then this word
filling the space between our mouths.
In itself, enough to explain what
pushes the earth from day into night.
What faith. What terror.

Justice

— after Lorna Crozier

I make important decisions with help
from a simple can of Alphagetti
by composing earth-shaking sales offers
in sauce-stained hues:
DEAR KELLOGG'S,
I WOULD LIKE TO SELL MY SOUL
FOR A LIFETIME SUPPLY OF FROOT LOOPS.
Other mornings, I aim for the Descartes-esque:
I CONSUME THEREFORE I AM.
Yes, the alphabet is making an all-caps comeback
à la Heinz and you can't blame the other
multinationals for elbowing in:
C for Coca-Cola Company;
F for Ford…
I'll admit it was my *J'adore Dior* T-shirt
that convinced me to attempt
to sell my name on eBay
for just enough venture capital
to buy a swirl cone at McDonalds.
Still, I'm getting better at owning what I say:
letter by letter, the bill
for my every word's exact worth
slowly adding up.

Temperance, or You'll never wear a tank top in this town again

Enamel? Gone. Fillings? Many. High-pitched ear squeal due to enhanced radiowave receptivity? Weekly if not daily if not every hour-on-the-hour coinciding with CFUN's not-so-fun hourly update brought to you in part by the kind folks at Colgate in co-operation with the Greater Vancouver Association for the Deaf. Nowadays I try to smile more than a Wal-Mart discount special because science has proven—at last—that a good make-out session makes my mouth water, flushing out plaque and preventing cavities and that's why 3 out of every 4 dentists now recommend sucking face. And although the Can-We-Get-Together Amendment to the I-No-Longer-Have-Drunken-Sex-With-Unattractive-Losers Bill was long since vetoed, I would sooner declare a locomotion (*come on, baby!*) than footnote this in honour of all my might've-beens-that-never-were[1]. It's true: my inability to withstand pain in hand-to-hand combat with flaming bat'leths has brought great dishonour to my family. Which is proportionately ten thousand times less important than the panic attacks caused by the probability of a mirth-filled, gift-toting senior citizen sliding down my chimney one night while I'm sleeping and my inherent fear of men named Paul.

[1] Most Klingon mating rituals involve combative foreplay.

Hope

What you fear most, giving
in to this feeling—
your stomach
a wet towel slowly wrung out
by cold hands—at an age
when you could clearly
know better. But still,
here you are again
staring at the onion
on your cutting board.
Peel it or don't bother.
Bite down hard.
Now do you understand?
With a dull knife, you could
fashion what's left, try
to make its heart take
another shape.
Challenge yourself.
A swan?
A salt-frosted rose?
Impose what you will.
Layered, it falls apart
under such exacting scrutiny
to the smallest of circles:
an inelegant mouth
speaking in tears.
It says, Stay.
It says, I'll tell you
whatever you want to hear.

Prudence, or The place where you think of your ex

A fallow field without limit,
without tractors, ploughs
or even a horse
twitching in the darkness.

A place where asphalt
thins to gravel and dust
under the prolonged tread of feet.

There's only one sound
and your ears stick to it:

cars forcing
air around them
on a distant road.

There's also a barbed wire fence

(which could be leaned on, leaned on
intermittently)

St. George the Dragon Slayer

"A powerful helper against evil forces affecting individual lives."

—the *Oxford Dictionary of Saints*

Intellect

transposition from George W. Bush's "World Can Rise to this Moment," February 6, 2003

In a last-minute game to show the world
that words still have meaning
a head was mounted on a truck
by scientists and was sent
hundreds of miles inland. Here
is the situation as we find it:
difficult intelligence challenges.
Those who accept its challenge
demand a careful presentation of facts.
Others, a weapon.

For Corporal Kelly Card

transposition from "President Bush Announces Combat
Operations in Iraq Have Ended," May 1, 2003

What's she got?
Training to lay roads,
restore hospitals and educate
all of their children.
A home in the harbour
of some other city. The ageless appeal
of a young woman. A decency
that turned idle men in uniforms
hostile on a cold night. Words
no device of man can remove:
to the captives, Come out—
and to those in darkness,
Be free. The belief
her government must already know
of hundreds of possible sites—
     Nineteen months
      in a single bunker
       below a school

      is what she got.

The Greatest War of the 21st Century will be the War Against Time

transposition from "President Signs Energy Policy Act,"
August 8, 2005

The day Ralphie's dog ate Pete Dominici's stock
policies and blacked out strategically by the back door
was the day news spread that experts, exhausted
by the prospect of unlocking vast amounts of now,
encouraged Americans everywhere to grab
a cup of coffee and report to federal authorities
if sand was found in or around their windows or appliances.
That night, minute hands began moving, forward
and backward, quick-like, with minds of their own.
Then terrorists released secret government plans that stated time
was already too strong and growing
stronger everyday. Like ex-cons on a hunt for cans,
no one could decide when to start. An attack
was needed, though problematic after words like "immediately"
became moot. The President wants to fall farther back.
Other world leaders tell him to spring forward.
So far his new daylight savings seem ineffective at best.
Decades may or may not be passing
as laboratories discover nothing can be done.
Terrifying, time's get-up-and-go simply ran out and went.

Albuquerque Barrio

transposition from "President Bush Meets with First-Time Homebuyers in NM and AZ," March 26, 2004

When you landed, the intended plenty
shrunk into one discouraging moment:
you fell to the ground and it met you like a husband,
shorelined you to this part of the world
permanently. Bright soil. No bushes.

No welcoming band to put a tear in the eye either.
The airplane returned to Mexico.
To reason the past three years went with it
seemed acceptable as the city crowds moved
backward under popping cables, junk everywhere.

Madmen on TV screens share terror.
The savings you had put aside were enough
to buy a telephone, yet your pockets
filled with ideas instead of quarters:
the role of the individual is to own a dream—

A house is like a cowboy hat,
good for courage, but in the end
practical as a relative in Mexico:
something to save money for,
then abandon when broke.

On Their Way to Wyoming, They Roam Around Iowa

transposition from "President Discusses AG Policy at Cattle Industry Convention," February 8, 2002

Theirs is such a relaxing pace.
"That's where Harry lives. He farms corn."
"He looks like he's pretty well settled in."
Down the road a little bit, Crawford says:
"Joe Nighthorse owns this—160 acres.
He farms soybeans. He's a fine, fine
god-fearing man."
Ann asks: "A shut-in?"
"His job is tougher than a hole."
She thinks about their land, asks, "Did it rain?"
and Crawford doesn't know how best
to manage it—"I was traveling
the farm one time with old Kenneth when
we hadn't been at this so long, and the first
thing I asked old Kenneth was 'where's
the water?' and, Ann, old Kenneth was explaining
like I should trim down—cut the new-growth
cedar because new-growth cedar, the pecans,
and oaks suck out a lot of water.
'Gimmickry,' I says
to old Kenneth and old Kenneth says,
'For those who work hard, it'll rain
all the time and there'll be hay enough
to feed all of us cows.'"

Real Estate

transposition from George W. Bush's State of the Union Address, January 29, 2002

Retired?
Worked hard and saved all your life?
Want a cleaner environment?
Hurry up and light that match—
other men and women are also running
from the centres of large cities
into their own, more remote jungles.
Need facts, videos, diagrams?
We've got 'em.
Our three goals:
Location! Location! Location!
The last time we met
deserts, caves, and mountaintops
were free. No longer.
Because of inflation, the price
of a vast ocean is now catastrophic—
thirty million a day for two decades.
So forget your debt.
Others are acting elsewhere.
In four short months, nothing
will be left.

Get Yourself Into It!

transposition from "President Bush Highlights Health and Fitness Initiative," July 18, 2003

Youngsters doing jumping jacks,
Olympic gold medallists—
All across our metroplex
the overstressed and overtaxed stay strong
in order to promote this latest fitness trend:
thirty minutes a day, five days a week,
a healthy body and a healthy mind
will earn you enough steak
to eat like a president.
Spread the message.
Eat steak and live a longer life.
It's the presidential challenge!
Are you always tired of being the little guy?
Had too much neighbourly small talk with ex-sports stars—
Good to see you, Rick, how's the fastball?
Rick always saying, "I want to put the word
out for running, how'd you do it nationally?"
What I always tell him:
"Friend, I ran hard and will run again,
and if you want to run after me,
you'll have to run harder until it doesn't
hurt anymore and keep on running.
You see, I, too, started with
nothing except a good pair of legs
because making the right choice in life
is exercise enough: you count the number
of states you can defeat and then
run to win."

Talking to Other Canadians About Canada

transposition from George W. Bush's Inaugural Address,
January 20, 2001

We all say thank you because we are
this story's author: a flawed and fallible
people taken root in one nation.
Our civility is a tactic and a sentiment.
Sometimes the most important tasks of love
are done by everyone.

He's Your Pusher

transposition from "President Bush Announces Drug Control Strategy," February 12, 2002

Drugs and you: a team…another kind of bottoms-up…so forget all this over-the-counter talk about "personal responsibility"…you are a fabulous mobster, hip to every down-the-hatch fad, and he trafficks the A-B-C basics better than a 280-metric ton Columbian cocaine cartel: E, K, GHB…and you know what happens after, in the chaos-flow…in groups, love your friends so much you become inseparable…make no mistake, find your dealer and tell him—on drugs—about the hippest presidential promise ever: *If It Feels Good Do It!*…then get to business…*we'll be "measured"—you'll "measure" for us first…and everyone will definitely drop "it" if we are…*

St. George and His Dragon

*transposition from "President's Remarks at Faith-Based and
Community Initiatives Conference." March 3, 2004*

He preached streetwise stem-twisters,
a wallet's worth of miracles
for the wonderless, stories
to lift the soul, knowing God
kept us alive for such a time as this.

We could risk the heroic
by fancifying angels with violet beams
of holiness and inhuman strength,
though never needed to: God was not
in our voice, God was
our voice.
    He said, "You never hear
half of what you listen to."

Was that faith then?

Half-heard or overheard, some radiance
in the inner ear acknowledging
what we've always wanted to know?

Hagiographies

"And what if all this land, all our life,
everything we see,
should turn into a book, a story,
and never turn back again?"

—Roo Borson,
Short Journey Upriver Toward Oishida

"Behold St. Christopher and go thy way in safety"

— a common inscription for St. Christopher medallions,
which are typically hung from the rear-view mirror of a car

Merging into everyone else
already on their way, already getting there
from side streets—other roads and their conjugations:
bushes in straight rows—to the unexpected
two-laned right turn, blood rush
and four-way flashers. In passing,
accidents have a certain elegance.
Slow-stop traffic under crowbar lampposts,
the daylight always just so
on the sunny bumpers between cars,
on the men at run towards a livestock trailer
tipped to the meridian, its own particular good morning
wounded across the grid-locked southbound, glint-silver
and bleeding hay—which drifts as all things do
after they spill out and, uncontained, go
to wherever it is they need to go.

For St. Jude, or What gets him where he is
   — after Joe Denham

Lists, cigarettes, his legs.
Fire hydrant, piss puddle, crack face, bus pole.
Weed.
Women, but mostly men.
Men with women.
Men with men.
A few cans of Colt-45, coat-stuffed and warming over with his every
footstep north.
Friday nights and forty bucks.
The fact men are out everywhere and he's just another one of them.
E—dry-swallowed or cut and railed up John A. MacDonald-style off
an apartment call box—and jittery jaw.
The undermind of words.
Self-reflexive questions like: where will I be when I get there?
A patois-talking, jibber-jabber OD-nutcase and her ability to vanish
leprechaun-like down alleyways.
Street signs.
Some kid his age, Tourette's-programmed into "Bud? Bud? Bud?"
selling street-corner dime bags from a zippered knapsack and a huskie
puppy howling into the foghorn, surf-broken night.

For St. Fiacre

went to the std clinic, told to come back in a week if nothing changes. it didn't go away. i didn't go back.
— *Blog entry by Anon. on www.someoneelse.com*

This story doesn't want to be touched.
This story is wounded and silent and dangerous
in its anonymity. This story is to be read and read only.
This story can be traced back further,
partner to partner until you discover
something greater than your own understanding of it
walking through your body and finding rest.
This is the story of a farm and a forest and a man with infinity
everpresent in his mind. This story is a long conversation
of pauses—between which anything can happen.
Like most anecdotes, this story will never tell you
what you really want to know: the name of the woman
sitting in the waiting room, crossing
and uncrossing her legs; the colour of the examination table;
whether or not you believe
other people's need will destroy you
long before your own.
This much is clear: early in the dusk of your thigh,
glowing in the midst of so much pink,
these almost moons must slip like apple seeds
under the fingertip and respond to your touch
by disappearing.

For the Anonymous Saint of Gaming
— *after Nick Thran*

For the unforgiving plastic of every light gun's
red trigger; for everyone who loves to toggle;
for the controller cord, plugged-in and kinked into coil, the final
link from here to anywhere else lifelike and almost living;
for every A-B-button joypad-swirl combination
attack-move that blistered thumbs in the Sunday morning
quiet of a half-lit basement. You know who
Mario and Luigi are, don't you? This is about
well-waxed moustachios, about brotherhood.
This is about Goombas, Koopas and Paratroopas.
This is about Nintendo, about the greatest plumbing
escapade known to modern man, how
that 8-bit bible's narrative undertones
have hard-wired your later life:
the Star Power, the Magic Mushrooms,
this affinity while under the influence of either
for smashing apart brick blocks with a single fist—
underworlds like late-night alleyways
that can only be escaped via pipe, like the green one
you hide in the cut-out pages of a second-hand novel
and smoke from in anticipation of the only
Game Over you've ever waited for: to be long gone
long before you know it.

For St. Christopher, or Outside a strip-mall Starbucks

The three of them drag two shipping flats each
from the loading bay behind the hardware store
to make jumps from a well-waxed sidewalk curb
by the green dumpster in a trellised alcove,
where earlier they left a bike and two longboards
between a shopping cart and a compost bin.
Below anti-theft floodlights, the boarders—
backs sloped and wind-slickered—stop
and stack the six crates. Next to a Lexus
in the parking-lot corner, they build a platform,
which they ignore then kick at
when the time for smashing finally comes.

For Veronica, Our Lady of Xerox

When the CEO wants a 250-page report
whittled down to 316 slides of raw data expressed
in bar graphs with one or two sexy
pie charts thrown in, all she hears is
<insert foghorn>
and gets straight to work.
Not the kind of woman who knew
what she wanted early on, in difficult times
she'll wear a sensible grey skirt, keep pretty
good company with men, keep pretty
good company with men, keep pretty
good company with me and sometimes love
Raymond, a mortgage broker from Illinois.
If you were picturing some
raven-haired maven terrorizing white-collar
Americans by credit card,
by floating-heart thought bubbles
while committing Page 4 capers—
Fashion Passion, First Date Fate—
at the speed of ZOOM!
in the ooh-la-laliest cartoon haute couture
$4 Canadian can buy, you're picturing
the wrong Veronica. Most mornings
at 9:15, you'll find her at the mailroom's
IR C6800 Colour Le Copier—
such precision! what clarity!—
selecting paper size then quantity before hitting
the copy button again and again and again.

For St. Jude

Trash everywhere around the garbage can
chained to the bus pole: silvery
candy wrappers, a sock, the stomped
rectangle of a smoke pack,
some broken glass.
                        In the nunnery graveyard
across the street, a man in silhouette
weeping against an angel
with no arms.
                        Waiting out the night,
this is where I begin too many
days to count, dawn like pepper in my eyes
as the streetlights turn off in unison, while real
or imagined, the cable-sparks of a trolley
crackle through the downtown, getting closer
and closer and closer to take me farther
east in a plush seat.
                        The man across the street
coughs.
          Waiting the night out, the last stars
are braille moving us through the blackness before
morning's brighter courtesies.

   Sunrise, sunrise—

For you he touches a hand
to his face.

   Sunrise, sunrise—

For you the bus dreams of me, waiting
on the bench for the 8 Eastbound, waiting
for the bus, any bus, but none
ever comes.

Creeping St. John's Wort, Late October

A voice in the snowdrift.

All afternoon, it sings
your praises when no one else
will listen, tells you
how to lie between
all that is frozen—
the fields, this meadow,
the embankment below the firs—
without vanishing into winter.

A ladder that separates
loss from longing:

green leaves climbing
from bright snow.

Grief, or St. Isidore roams the Stanthorpe Farming District

Drift to one faraway stand of dry eucalyptus
then all the way back to the same silver-barked pines
over rippled soil and kicked-apart piles of weeds,
a marathon back and forth, hunching, picking
the field in gloves whiter than a debutante's
as the courgettes underfoot fall in armloads
into rucksacks and pails: just twist, rip,
move on.

St. Erasmus in the Gulf

Jailed, though this time so far from land
there will be no raven with a small desert
between its beak to sustain him, just
letters from the last supply ship, his solitude
sailing between their every line. Here, his mouth
forms an observance of duty. Above him,
a freak jargon of light: blue flame
like a star-flare around the slowly turning
radar and a birthmarked crescent moon.
It was the other details that made war
easier to believe in. The ship's gun
pointed him nowhere. On deck,
his face was the colour of a face at sea.

What God Asked of Joan in the Fields of Orléans

Suppose my mouth holds everything you ever wanted.
I speak like a finger tracing ribs.
I say, Rest.
Is this defeat then?
This one soft word blown across your face?

Is this not what you meant when you asked to be held?
Walls to be pushed against?
The comfort of a distant trumpet, your head
an envelope for its terrible song?

Either way, don't I offer the end of all things tender?
A heart like a fenceless field, then nightfall, men on horses
careening through burnt grass, these hooves
a mute vibration passing through your bones.

I speak and moths fly off like snapping fingers.
Half-shadow and half-sound, I say,
Follow me down the river.
I will be the arrow.
You will be my mark.

Saints & Patronages

St. Anthony of Padua
lost articles; seekers of lost articles; oppressed people

St. Brendan
mariners; sailors; watermen; whales
Brendan and his brothers figure in *Brendan's Voyage*, a tale of monks
traveling the high seas of the Atlantic, evangelizing to the islands,
possibly reaching the Americas in the 6th century

St. Christopher
bachelors; motorists; skateboarders; taxi/truck drivers; travelers

St. Erasmus
danger at sea; mariners; navigators; sailors; storms
Namesake for the static electric discharge called Saint Elmo's Fire

St. Fiacre
venereal disease

St. George
chivalry; England; poverty; soldiers; against evil

St. Isidore
farm workers; farmers; labourers; rural communities

St. Joan of Arc
captives; France; martyrs; prisoners; rape victims; soldiers

St. John's Wort
a homeopathic cure for depression

St. Jude
desperate situations; forgotten causes; impossible causes; lost causes

St. Veronica
laundry workers, photographers

"Temperance, and prudence, and justice,
and fortitude, which are such things as men can have
nothing more profitable in life."
— Wisdom 8:7

"So faith, hope, love remain, these three;
but the greatest of these is love."
— Corinthians 13:13

Acknowledgements

The epigraphs throughout are drawn from: *Meadowlands* by Louise Gluck (New York: Ecco, 1996); *Sweet Machine* by Mark Doty (New York: HaperPerrenial, 1998); *Oxford Dictionary of Saints* by David Hugh Farmer (New York: Oxford University Press, 1998); *Short Journey Upriver Toward Oishida* by Roo Borson (Toronto: McClelland & Stewart, 2004); and *The Holy Bible*.

The epigraph from "In Praise of Letting Go" is drawn from my mother's personal journals.

"St. Brendan and the Abbot of Clonmacnoise" owes a debt to "Lightenings viii" by Seamus Heaney.

Let's face it: this book and many others wouldn't be possible without the support of the Canada Council for the Arts. Thanks to Paul Seesequasis and everyone else involved. I also want to thank the Queenswood Centre and the Sisters of Saint Ann. If they hadn't let a smart-mouthed twenty-something know-it-all harass them on Saturday mornings, you wouldn't be reading this now.

Thanks also to Shannon, Lindsay, and Anthony Horlor along with all my friends for their continual support over the years it took me to write this. And thanks to Jody Lesiuk and Shannon Horlor (again) for their feedback on earlier drafts of this manuscript. Darren Michael St. Laurent: all bullshit aside, you helped these final drafts get where they are (yeah, you did) and I'm grateful for it.

"In Praise of Beauty" won 1st place in the poetry category in the 2006 Great Canadian Literary Hunt. "Intellect" was shortlisted in the poetry category in the 2003 Great Canadian Literary Hunt.

"St. Brendan and the Isle of Sheep" was an Editor's Choice for *Arc*'s 2006 International Poem of the Year contest.

Earlier versions of the poems in *Saint George the Dragon Slayer* were published by Mosquito Press in 2003 in a chapbook titled *Our Mission, Our Moment.* Earlier versions of the poems in *Hagiographies* won an honourable mention in Frog Hollow Press's 2003 Chapbook Contest.

I would also like to thank the editors of *Event, THIS Magazine, Pine Magazine, Arc, The Malahat Review,* and *Seminal: The Anthology of Canada's Gay Male Poets* where some of these poems were or will be published.

I owe a debt to many writers, especially those I've worked with, those whom I studied under and those who've promoted me over the years, including: Matt Rader, Billeh Nickerson, Aislinn Hunter, Don McKay, Roo Borson, Derk Wynand, Helen Humphreys, Pat Lane and Lorna Crozier.

Thank you to Karen Haughian and Tara Seel at Signature Editions.

Lastly, to John Barton, my editor: thank you for your wit, thoroughness, and belief in me. *Made Beautiful by Use* is, in fact, exactly that thanks to your efforts.